ChandelierHead

ChandelierHead

Grace Storm

Published by Grace Storm, 2024.

CHANDELIERHEAD

First edition. March 22, 2024.

Copyright © 2024 Grace Storm.

ISBN: 979-8224709656

Written by Grace Storm.

Table of Contents

ChandelierHead

As I sat basking in the heat of the flames that
engulfed my thoughts
and each one like shards of glass multiplied until
they filled my eyes with ill will,
I saw a figure in the window
Or rather, a reflection.

So I turned to look at the door behind me.
Which unfortunate drunken party guest dared to stumble upstairs and
past my room's door?

I got up, but on a closer inspection, no one seemed to be
there
and there were no sounds of footsteps...

I resumed burrowing into my half moon chair, trying
to block out the sounds of laughter below me
Whooping and screeching and singing off-key

God only knows what they were up to—
but thank God I wasn't down there.
Thank God I had the superior company
of an old book.

I scoffed.
But no, it was really quite sad.
They all lacked exposure to masterpieces like these—
— I licked my finger to turn the page —
they lack the knowledge to understand them
perhaps they lack the care

All they know how to do
is mock me for my clothing and my
vocabulary, which I'm forced to
dumb down for their sakes
Little do they know that I, too
mock them.

But why waste time even thinking of them.
I was ready to read.

But my eyes had barely begun scanning the text for
my place
when something like music
drifted into the room.

It wasn't the thumping, electric music from the party
It gently strolled in
lonely, yet seductive
subtly, yet it commanded all of my attention.

I rose from my seat, squinting as if to see it
dancing through through the air in a thin, blue ribbon
it sounded like smoke
like a stream.

I followed it to the window,
then something shifted outside.

"Oh no," I thought, *"some wretch clambered onto the roof of the porch, and they're playing Celtic flute."*

That wasn't a far fetched conjecture, as it had happened once before.
Well, minus the Celtic music, of course.
So I stepped one final determined step and threw the window open.

"Who's there?" I demanded. "Can't I have a sliver of peace?
I have classes in the morning, and unlike you, I choose to study."

The music stopped abruptly,
Something scraped and shuffled against the shingles.
One slid off and was sent toppling towards the ground
A shape shifted in the dead darkness,
then revealed itself in the faint lamplight from my bedside table.

A man
Standing,
Towering over me.

I staggered back; there was nothing between us now but the window screen—
hardly a protective barrier.

The man bent down, showing his awful face
it was young, and strangely appealing
yet undeniably horrid

It was blue, it was slimy, it was
dirty and staring and smiling,
with two red eyes
wide and glowing
like a car's tail lights.

My dry mouth gaped, letting out no words and no scream.
My face flushed with blood and adrenaline.

I took in every detail of the creature
from his platinum hair to his dirty blue robes
the pan pipe in his hand
the chandelier on his head
that he wore like a crown with pride and dignity

Every inch of him
dripped
with
water
and
mud

as if he'd just emerged from a swamp.

"Oh—
my God—" I stammered,
no louder than a whisper

I wanted to close the window with every part of my soul, but how could
I bear to get closer once more to that face?
With its neon turquoise skin like an old copper statue
Teeth so straight and unnervingly white—

That set of glistening teeth opened,
and out of the monsters mouth snaked my name

My name

softly, somehow
so familiar,
my own name

"Morana."

My head swirled.
I took off my glasses and rubbed my eyes.
Perhaps I had gone mad.
Perhaps I was high.

I opened my eyes again to the sight of the man— the *thing* — at my window
I backed up, keeping my eyes on him.
I couldn't turn around until I felt the door at my fingertips.

"Morana,"
the man or beast or ghost repeated,
his smile now gone and his red, watery eyes large.
They pleaded with me to stay.
So I stopped.

I reached behind me to prepare for a quick escape, should it be needed.
I pushed my fingers through the gap between the doorframe.

"What are you?" I asked.

"You mean,
who am I?"

An unplaceable accent tinged his pronunciation.

"No. When I say something, I mean it. *What,* I repeat, *are you?*"

He adjusted his chandelier crown and plucked a strand of seaweed from it.
The crystals showered droplets of water
shifting, casting speckles of orange light across his face.

"My dear,"
he said,
"My dear girl,
I am a friend."

I answered with silence and then a scowl.
"A friend?" I scoffed. "Most certainly not."

"My dear Morana, I assure you
it is
certainly so.
Though you do not know me,
I
know you."

A chill ran down my back.

The creature continued in his silk-like voice,

"You come to the graveyard on warm afternoons
You sit on the grass, or on
the bench by the church

You wander the tombs
the stones
and the trees
You recite poetry, and write
on loose sheets of paper
or in that little brown notebook
you always carry."

His tone became
Wistful.

"Sometimes you don't write or read at all, well—
you just read the names
on the stones as you pass by them
alone, in the warm sunlight
It reflects off your funny round glasses
and once in a while at just the right angle

and just the right time—
the light gets caught in your hair
melting it into browns and golds, more like your eyes and less like those
plain black clothes
you always wear."

His voice dropped a little.

"Those brown eyes look so sad
as you pass by each name on each stone.

You look at your feet, knowing underneath
lie bodies long dead

long buried,
long vacant,
wanting of souls."

He paused.

"You wish you could believe in souls."

His blue fingertips paled as he pressed them against the screen.

"You have no faith in spirits, or in angels, or in gods,
yet you call out 'God!'
while acting out old plays
But they're not just sonnets to you, they're real
they're your words too

and I see
how it feels
when you mention that name

half expecting someone to answer.

Do you wish
someone would?"

His eyes told me he was listening for my answer.
I couldn't say a thing. But it didn't matter.
I didn't have to.

"It breaks your heart," he said.
"... that you believe in nothing and no one.

You know you'll die, and have no idea of what's waiting for you.
You see everyone in your life as walking corpses,
wasting their lives, comforting each other with the promise of heaven
never even considering
the things you consider.

You wish you could ignore it too.

Instead it disgusts you that they live every day so unaware of their own
mortality
so you live in mourning clothes.

Mourning your future death
and the deaths of those around you.

You painted your room black to prepare yourself for the darkness
of the nonexistent afterlife

This house is so full of people and life—
but you are

Seperated from them
and the sounds of their laughter
only remind you.
So you withdraw further.

Somewhere quiet.
a place where
the surroundings reflect the contents
of your mind.
To spend time with the only one who understands.

He pulled his hand back and tilted his head.

"When I saw you in the graveyard, I wondered if you were always so alone."

He waited for my reply, but none arrived.

"So,"
he said,
"I followed you home."

I retreated even farther, leaning my back against the door.

"Demon," I said, "or ghost, or vision, answer me: what are you?
What manner of being speaks with me now,
and tells me the thoughts in my heart?"

He drew back, looking hurt, so I lowered my voice.

"You say you see me at the graveyard—are you one of the dead?
How do you know me so deeply?
Why do you call yourself my friend?
And what is that ridiculous thing on your head?"

He smiled just a hint of a smile,
so gentle and pure,
with something in his eyes like admiration,
or something more.

"Come with me."

I blinked.

"Come with me,"
he repeated.
"And I'll give you
the answers you seek."

My fear shed from me like a snake's skin,
trust replacing all my doubt.

I knew it then:
this is what I've been waiting for.

Mr. Pathetic

How pathetic.
Look at him, there—
careless, sluggish,
arrogant, pretentious
Enough chin for three people
enough sarcasm for the both of us.
The silver clip on his tie alone
costs more than I could hope to scrounge together in a year.

And look at that scowl, now,
just who does he think he is?
The floppy skin around his nostrils scrunching up
That's the face of a man who's never tasted cheap wine.

Tapping on his desk with an—
(need I even say it?)
an obnoxiously expensive pen
My eyes linger there
then wander over the desk,
over a useless gold plated pocket watch with the chain resting in a spiral
and land finally
on a similarly metallic picture frame
turned away from me.

I take it.

It's a nice little frame,
friendly,
(unlike *him*.)
The sort you find in your grandparents house
lightweight, inexpensive, but old
and it surrounds a photo of young people

but it's in black and white, so somehow the young faces staring back
appear older.

I recognize one of the men as the younger brother to Mr. Pathetic
The second is advanced in age, maybe a grandfather or uncle
But the boy
in the center
I can't help but stare...

His stunning smile is
humorous,
mischievous

But sort of sweet
sort of... nice.

A cousin to the man sitting across from me?
Strange, to think if they're related.
They must've turned out so differently.

Mr. Pathetic clears his throat.
I look at him. "What."

Mr. Pretentious extends a hand expectantly.

I slap the picture into his palm, then I reach for another frame.

Mr. Pompous chuffs,
"Young lady, what do you want with my family photographs?"
His voice is like the smell of leftover food stuck in the sink drain.
Expired milk sloshing out of the jug.

I look back at him with a matching distasteful expression.

"I'm bored," I say.

"Too bad," he says.

Well, too bad for him
I grab the picture anyway.

And there's the same boy again—
older,
handsomer
but wearing a slightly different smile.
Something is present now
that wasn't before, or
maybe something left.
He's a little less confident.
A little more angry.

Oh.
Well, shit.
I probably should've seen it the first time.

"You and your brother?" I ask,
pointing at the photo.

He nods as if it's obvious.
I guess it was.
But now I feel gross all over.

I whack the picture face down on the desk.

"Just what do you think you're doing?"

His voice is sharp
sour, like an ancient piano.

I sniff and shrug,
wondering how that young man turned into... this?
How that pretty face
got so distorted
Crushed
into a greasy prune
a milkshake left in a hot car for hours...
Boated. Infected. Rancid.

He clears his throat. "I asked you a question."

"A rhetorical question."

"Don't you get smart with me."

"Sorry." (I don't mean it.)
"I'm in a bad mood."

"Aren't you always?"

I pause. "Sure."

Silence.

"...You looked really different."

"Hm?" He doesn't grace me with eye contact.

"In the pictures."

He doesn't give me the privilege of an answer.

"You looked a whole lot better."

He throws down his paperwork and rubs his face with vigor.
"Let's see how good you'll look in thirty years."

I must've made him mad, because he was the first to speak after another pause.
"You know, with an attitude like yours, you'll age worse than I have."

I laugh. I laugh bitterly.

"I'm not in any way being funny."
His black eyes shoot up at me and strike me dead silent.
"Take a good hard look at what you'll be, one day."

I lean over his desk,
invade his space,
place my sweaty hand on the varnished wood
and take a deep breath.

I want to say something that will hurt him.
Something that will sting.

"I'll never be anything like you."

But
that's more defensive than offensive.

He isn't even fazed.

My blood boils.
The fluid in my eyes boils.

He wears an ugly expression on his already unpleasant face,
but he isn't upset.
He twirls his flashy pen between his fingers.

I hate the Freemason ring on his pinky.
I hate his cologne that stinks like a closet of old clothes.
I hate the way he always looks at me
as if my IQ is below forty.

He finally sucks in a breath through his nose.
"You hate my money,
my position,
the way I look,
the way I talk.
But I'm nothing special— you hate everything.
And the same goes for me.
I hate *everything,* and you're no exception.
So, if you think you'll never be anything like me, you're wrong.
Because, young lady, you already are."

                                I just sort of sat there. Not saying anything.

For the first time in God only knows how long, I can't bring myself to
argue.
(And I argue just for the sake of it. I argue just to argue, even when I
know that I'm wrong.)

I wish I had some snappy reply.
I wish I didn't see young eyes in an old face.
I wish I'd never have to look at that face again.

So, I sit.
I wait,
hoping desperately to think of something to say
But that moment never comes.

There's the sound of a pen on paper
a ticking clock
faintly, outside, cars in the rain.

And I never get around to saying another thing.

"ALAN VALENTINE" or, Val, to me

Alan is a no good nobody.
That much I've come to accept.
He's a bottom of the barrel
Short end of the stick
Dick.
Who likes to think he's the It.

He lives like he's the pearl of his oyster world
He smiles like he's the son of God
And when all eyes are on him
—that's roughly all times, if you'll believe it—
He loves to look at me and rub it in

I was convinced I loved him
I was obsessed with him, in any case
I even could've sworn he felt the same for me
Anyway... at some point
I realized that was ridiculous.

When you love Val
You don't love a person
You love a whole damn solar system
Orbiting,
Tossed about his center of gravity
At his fingertips
At his whim.

When I finally saw Val
Saw him for what he really, truly is? Well—
You can't reason with that level of narcissism
He shut me down at every fork in the conversation

Sure. Maybe I don't have tact.
But I'd rather confront things as they are
All fifty two cards face up on the floor
When we can see the problem
Then we can solve it

Val doesn't appreciate that.
Oh, he lives in high towers if his mind's own making—
Safe and protected from all that
In spite and spiteful of all that
All that would ever fix the issue
All that makes him tick is praise, applause, and more praise
And that's it!

And that's it, I guess.
I've said my piece.
I'd love to say someday he'll come crawling back to me, but of course
Pride would ever prevent his knees
Getting dirty.

So when you see that shining light on your TV
Recall this scene in your mind's eye:
Alan Valentine
At the sight of the crime
Being briefed as to what went down
Then before saying one word to me,
As I laid in the streets,
He asked cameraman number three
To check if his receding hairline
Was looking awful noticeable today.

Naw, Val,

You look great.

Uncle Mickey

25

I made it to the house and Mickey was in a state
like I'd never seen him
20 pizza boxes open around the living room
And he was wearing some sort of getup
glam rock studded jumpsuit that would make Elton John jealous
which didn't jive at all with his semi professional haircut

I said, "My God, uncle Mick! What is this, your last night on earth?"
I had to yell over Riverdale blaring on the TV
as I grabbed the remote to shut it off with one hand, and with the other
balanced the paper bag of Chinese takeout
that I'd spent good money on, but was now obviously
unnecessary

He grumbled and squirmed across the couch to steal it back, and when
he succeeded, pressed the volume button, didn't let go, and let it soar
I had to drop the food. I had to cover my ears.
"Are you okay???"
He sprawled out lazily and answered,
"Rose, something something something."
"What?"
"Rose, I'm having a splentastic night!"
"Splentastic?" I repeated.
And that's when I knew something had gone awry in his mind.

"Uh, you're scaring me," I said.
I had to read his lips to catch the words, "everything's fine,"
but it didn't console me,
not one iota
not one bit.

"Will you turn this damn thing down! I can't hear you!"

I had a look in my eye that told him: no more messing around.
His face went blank like a guilty dog. He fumbled to turn the TV off.
Snap.
It left the room a little darker.

I stared him down,
down there on the couch.
I don't think he liked that;
me being taller.
So he sort of over-adjusted, tugging at the stretchy blue pants, trying to
get as comfortable as possible
Trying to prove something to me?

"Want to finally take that trip to Hoboken?" He asked.
Again alarms went off in my mind.
Weeoo weeoo. He's lost it.
"Tell me what happened," I said.
A sad smile.
He sat up
He slapped his knees before standing.
Then began the pacing.

He scratched his neck behind that big bejeweled collar. Dandruff
scattered from his conspicuously box dyed black hair.
At last, he looked at me— and pulled in a bit too close—
"What would you do—"
Pizza breath.
"If I told you—"
His brown irises hovered in the center
of the whites of his eyes
like UFO's
"That I had done something—"

More pizza breath.
"Really not-good?"

I winced.
I tried to sound as gentle as possible.
"I'd... believe you."

He backed up. (thank God.)
"You usually do believe me." He picked up a pizza box off the coffee table
presented it to me
as an offering.
Vinegar from the disgraceful buffalo chicken stung my nose.
"No, thanks," I said, and pointed to the Chinese food
that was leaking general Tso's sauce onto his carpet.

He took notice of it but didn't care. "Oh, right." He shoved three slices
at once into his mouth.
Greasy chunks dropped back into the box.
"Eat," he urged
with a very clogged up and muffled voice.

Well,
I thought,
okay, might as well.

I went into the tiny
untidy kitchen and
arranged the food on the yellow countertop.
He followed me
which was good, I didn't want to leave him alone.
He opened the fridge as I pulled apart the wooden chopsticks
picked up some crab rangoon
and put them on the only clean plate I found in the dish drainer
it was the one I'd painted for him, at the pottery studio
it had Coraline on it.
I covered her button eyes with fried rice.
Since the fridge was still open, I put the boxed up leftovers inside.

Mickey poured me a ginger ale without asking,
he knew it was my favorite
and for himself, you know
Mickey took the whole two liter bottle

then he followed me back to the living room.
In silence I took the remote from the crack in the couch cushions and
turned the TV back on.
Riverdale resumed in the middle of a teenage makeout scene, yippee
I don't think Mickey got any more interest out of it than I did, it was just
noise to fill the void
for me it was noise to cover up
the sound of my chewing
It always felt necessary, I guess that's the effect
of growing up
with YouTube.

Eventually, unintentionally
I became wrapped up

in the storyline
and even after I was done eating, placing my plate aside
I curled up
with the scratchy throw blanket and leaned on the singular decorative
pillow
with sequins embroidered into it that stabbed my ear and cheek (I could
imagine the pattern of little dents in my skin)
and I watched the episode through to the end.

As the credits rolled into a commercial break, we made no comment on
the show
Mickey was devouring two more slices rolled up like a taco.
And I was like, "Geez," I said, "Aren't you going to puke if you have much
more of that?"

He shook his head rapidly. "Nah."
He spoke through the side of his mouth.
"I have a technique— you have to space 'em out over time.
It's like drinking alcohol."

I was a little disturbed.
I sat up straight.
"But why? Why would you do that?"
He didn't answer.
He took a swig of soda.
"Rose," he said.
"Yeah?"

He wasn't looking at me, but
addressing someone by their name is more than enough
acknowledgment.
It felt significant.

I wondered if he was going to tell me
the
really-not-good
thing
he had done.

But he only asked a question.
"Why'd you come over tonight?"
I reached for my phone in my pocket. "I told you I was going to—I
texted you, don't you remember?"
"No, I remember, I mean,"
He stopped mid sentence
I checked the time
on my phone
9:49
no notifications
then I looked back up at him.
"What?" I asked quietly.

His face might've been dazed or he might've been in thought
either way I was concerned
but I trusted.
At least I was trying really hard to trust.
He rubbed his mouth, creating wrinkles.
"I mean, like, why."

I leaned forward to see his face better.
"Because I missed you."
That finally got a bit of a smile out of him I think,
it was hard to tell, he was hiding it with his hand.
"So. Tell me," I said.
I saw his face shift, he was dreading this

"What did you do?"

"Something bad," he said simply.
"What, did you kill someone?"
He chuffed through his nose; something that I assumed was a laugh.
"So go ahead, then," I bade. "I'm not gonna judge."
"Mn-m. You wouldn't forgive me for this one."
So it *was* serious.
"Well, that depends, I mean..." I looked earnestly at him, but he still wouldn't meet my eyes.
"Why did you do it?"
He thought for barely a second before blurting—
like he'd had more than enough time to think it over before—
"I hate my life."

Was I supposed to say something?
"Oh..."
"...why?"
He snorted. "What is there to like?"

"I," I stuttered, "I think there's a lot of things to appreciate."
I came up with a few on the spot,
I thought that should help him,
and it wasn't too hard.
"You've got a nice house."
"Barely," he interrupted.
"Hey, let me finish. You've got a house, a car, super awesome, uh... clothes,"
(Where *did* he find that outfit?)
"You're kinda young-ish, aren't you?"
He shook his head no.
"Well, you're not old. And you look good, and you're gay—"

He laughed. "Being gay doesn't do crap for me."
"Makes you cooler."
"You *would* say that."
"Shut up, I'm not done. Here's a good one: you're really smart. You're like the smartest person I know. *And*,"
This was my big finale
"You have the perfect job."

His face sank.
He was silent.
Whoops. I screwed that up.
I lowered my voice. "You... don't?"
"Nope." He popped the P.
I got even quieter. "Did you quit?"
He just nodded.

It was at NASA.
That was the job.
I didn't know what specifically, but something important.
I figured maybe I just wasn't smart enough to understand
why on earth someone would quit that,
but after all, I'm no rocket scientist.

I gave him the benefit of my ignorance.
"That's not bad, is it. You can probably take your pick of jobs now, with that on your résumé."
He shook his head. "That's not the bad thing I did. It's only part of it."
I scoffed. "I don't understand. Why can't you tell me?"

I watched him.
I saw his wheels turning.
He looked up at the ceiling,

as if to heaven, as if saying a wordless prayer or
asking forgiveness or
looking for an answer
or remembering

It was such a profound expression, I expected something grand to come
out of his mouth,
but being Mickey,
he turned to me and said,
arm leaning against the backrest,
"You know Breaking Bad?"

I wanted to laugh, but he was deadly serious.
"Are you cooking meth now?"
"No, nonono. It's... it's like this. D-did you watch the show? I gotta
know."
"Um, not really, only an episode here and—"
"Okay, I'll explain it. So, Walter White, right, he's the main guy. He's a
failure and no one respects him, and he hates his life but he just settles,
because that's what he's expected to do.
But he finds out he has cancer, and he's like, I gotta do something about
this!"
He looked at me desperately.
I tried to find the common thread.
"You're not sick, are you?" I asked.
"No, I just..."
He sighed.

He slumped back into the cushions.
Changed his mind,
twisted around a few times
and searched by swinging his arm

around the side
of the couch to find the ginger ale
tipped it back and polished it off
half turned to me once more and said,
"I just realized...
This has to stop."

"What does?"
"Me." He covered his mouth and burped. "Me, *me*— I have to stop. I have to stop being like this."
"Like what? I don't get it. You're not a failure, Mick, you're doing just fine. I'd kill to have the things you have." I paused. "Not literally."
"Yes I am a failure. But I'm a clever failure, that's the sad thing. I'm all wasted potential. I am Walter White."
I laughed
a real laugh with my whole chest. "You are not Walter White!"
He laughed too,
and then both of us together.
He knew he was being ridiculous.
It was good to see him smile
For the first time that night without
looking deranged
or trying to suppress it.
He pressed his fingertips into his forehead
and gave up on complaining.

I checked my phone again for no good reason.
"Are you going home?" He asked.
"No." I put it away. "Do you want me to?"
"No."
He glanced out of the corner of his eye. "Want dessert?"
I thought I should probably decline.

But hey, when the offer stands.
"What do you have?"

A moment later we were in the kitchen again
discovering treats packed in the freezer
under the dim orange light.
He handed me boxes of popsicles,
fished a loose double triple deluxe caramel magnum whatever bar from
behind the bags of frozen vegetables
then announced, "That's the stuff"
when he found the tub of mint chocolate chip.

With all the options present, he asked,
"Okay, which?"
Regrettably I had my eye on two choices.
"Umm... can I have more than one?"
He smiled and snapped his fingers. "Good thinking. Why should we
have to pick?"
I grabbed my selected items
kicking myself in the ass for being a self-destructive-junk-food-cravings
enabler.

I was sitting on the counter, and he was leaning against the sink
listening to the faint TV mumble from the other room
and the clinking of our spoons
against the ice cream bowls.
"You know," I said at length. "I'm pretty sure the moral of Breaking Bad
is supposed to be something like... 'don't let your ego get the best of you.'"
Mickey swallowed. "I thought you didn't watch it."
"I just heard that somewhere."

He waited a while before answering.
"I don't have an ego."
"I mean, we all do, technically."
"Er, not a bad one. I'm not..."

"Egotistical?" I finished for him.

"Uhuh. I'm *not*," he further emphasized.

"Not ever?"

He took an extra large bite to stall. "Mm...
Sometimes."

I hopped off the counter.

I reached behind him to toss my bowl in the sink.

"But I don't think that's why I'm like...

...

this."

As he said that, my elbow was resting on the edge of the sink

right where his back met the counter

I could feel his voice so close

it gave his words a different weight.

I stood in front of him.

"Why you're like what?"

He looked at me with sad eyes.

No longer flying saucers

Meteors

ever falling downwards.

"Uncle Mick?"

"Yeah?"

"Do you hate yourself?"

"...

...

Yeah."

A fog fell away from his face.
Something that had been cutting him off from the world
fortressing him away from
everything.

Now that the truth was out,
the cat out of the bag, the can of worms opened, the beans spilled
there was room for a new emotion.
One that I had witnessed
and felt
all too many times.
One that I would know anywhere
on any face.

It was shame.

I cringed inside, like,
for some reason, as if it were me,
as if he were a mirror
I knew it all too well, I could hardly bear to see it
The shrinking, trembling, hyper perceived
self awareness.

And yet stillness.

Knowing you're seen.

But I think shame is a sort of freedom.
When you're at your lowest
when you're at your grossest
when you feel stupid, and all too real

when you're at your most human
The worst thing you can do at a time like that
is hide your face.

He wanted to,
that was obvious.
But he didn't. He sat in it,
in that uncomfortable
itchy silence
and allowed me to see him.

If only I could've told him
I wanted to tell him
that none of it mattered to me.

I gave him the courtesy of backing up.
And because the silence was too long, I babbled whatever came to mind.
"I heard somewhere that hating yourself is the same thing as narcissism."
He let out a weak breath. "Awesome," he said, to let me know how helpful
I was being.
"I'm sorry. I don't know where that came from. Don't listen to me."
Embarrassed, I unwrapped a fudgesicle.
"I mean, you could be right. Where'd you hear it?"
I shook my head. "No. Doesn't matter."
(Internet.)

I started over, "Who told you to feel like that?" I said
(what I should've said in the first place.)
"Huh?" His voice was watery and shy.
I bit the fudge bar. "Who taught you to, you know... hate yourself."
He scratched his neck. "I don't know, I mean, I dunno what you mean.
Isn't that just something you do?"

"It couldn't have been like that forever. It has to come from somewhere."
"How do you know?"
"I— I, well, 'cause I feel like that too."

He exhaled and slouched. "You do?" He asked a little too enthusiastically, as if relieved.
I half smiled.
He became self aware. "Sorry I said it like that."
"That's okay. And yeah, I do,
I don't know if it's exactly the same as you feel,
but I'm mad at myself a lot, and disappointed, and...
I guess I don't exactly like myself all the time."
He nodded, asking me to continue.
"But I wasn't always so angry at myself. I learned it."
"Where from?"
"Other people. Family." I lifted myself onto the counter again. "Friends, even."
"Oh, yeah. Friends," he said in a spacey tone,
looking like he'd recalled a forgotten concept.
"You know, I didn't have those when I was your age. Not real ones. Because college... college wasn't fun."

I couldn't answer at first because I got tooth freeze.
I closed my eyes and waited for it to go away.
"Mm," I said when I could finally focus enough, "Yeah, well, you went to college young, right?"
He rolled his eyes. "Yeahhh. I wasn't a prodigy or anything, things just worked out like that."
"But you were, kind of. You were extra smart."
He frowned. He bit his thumbnail.
Tore it. Spit the piece into his fingers and flicked it.
Ew.

"I'm not smart. I just know how to do things."
I laughed, exasperated. "That's what being smart means."
He scrunched his nose. "*You're* smart, and you don't do *anything*."
I stopped and gaped.
He had a point.
Did he?
Was I?
"Uh... thanks?" I said.

He slid down the cabinets and sat on the floor.
I was taller again.
"Yeah," he said. "I hated people calling me smart. I don't want to be. That's the whole reason I didn't have friends back then, because that's all I was. Just smart."
I wrapped the popsicle stick in a napkin. "I don't know. Maybe it's just because you were younger."
He stared at the floor tiles. "That's not much better."
"It's true, though. College students want to be drinking and partying. You can't do that with a fifteen year old."
His brow creased. "I..."
My heart fell a little for that younger version of him.
I could see that kid in his face.
He sniffed. "Didn't think about it like that."

I checked my phone once more.
10:34
Wow how time gets sucked down the drain
when you're looking at something else.
"I hate that," he said.
The phone went back in my pocket,
and I observed a new rage growing in him.
"I should've been normal."

I shook my head. "Don't say that."
"Why can't I say it?" He looked up at me. "I should've been."
"I don't mean this as an insult, but you were a kid. You didn't have a choice to be normal or not. None of us do when we're young."

His dark brows lowered and seemed
to darken the rest of his face
"You keep saying it's not my fault, but it is.
I made my life the
way it is
and no one else is to blame.
It would be nice, though, wouldn't it? If I could put the responsibility on someone else? But I can't,
Rose,
that's not reality,
and you think this way because you're young, but you'll grow out of it when you make a few more mistakes."
I whispered quietly, "hey,"
I can't say for sure if he heard it.

"Do you want to know the real reason why no one in the family talks to me? No one but you? Did I ever tell you?"
He looked at me, but he wasn't looking at me, he was looking at himself with anger—
Or worse, disgust.
I shook my head.
"Fourteen years ago when my ex wife and I divorced, I couldn't be normal about it, I had to make it everyone's problem,
I had to tell them *why*.
Told my brothers and sisters.
It even got around to my son, which is why he doesn't talk to me now.
And then when my dad found out... I mean, your grandfather..."

Oh no.
By the way my grandfather talked about Mick, there was no surprise
that...
"All hell broke loose, you know what I'm saying," Mick said.
"I should've kept my mouth shut. I shouldn't have been so selfish. But I
just had to go
and let everyone know."

I didn't think it was selfish to tell them what he did.
He let out a bitter laugh. "And it gets worse!
When I didn't have a job,
and the court case and the child support and the alimonies
kicked me out on my ass,
Mick the embarrassment went crawling back,
guess where? to his parents,
to plead with them to rescue me out of the pit that I got myself into.
They helped—"
He shrugged.
"I mean, my mom helped. For a while. Gave me more than I deserved
and more than I expected.
But generosity runs out— and when she couldn't even put up with it
anymore, I went to my siblings. Took and took until every last one
couldn't stand me. Your parents, too—"
He looked at me
apologizing?
"Six years ago. That was the last time.
And now I might be doing— how did you put it earlier? 'Just fine?'
well it's not good enough when you can't repay anyone."

I whispered—
I don't know why I felt like I should.
"Money?"

He grunted and got up off the floor.
I stayed seated on the counter of course.
"Not just money," he answered.
I tried to imagine what he meant.
Places to stay?
Food?
A job?
Just someone to be there with him?
I couldn't convince myself
that he was bad enough to not deserve those things.

He leaned both forearms on the fridge
his forehead in them.
"I'm so scared. Because I did it again."
He sighed.
"I did it again, I always do this."
I shook my head. "What did you do?"
"I ruined everything again. Instead of working harder and being better,
I give up—
I throw out everything I have.
And now there's no one left who still cares, there's no one to help me if it
gets as bad as it did."
His voice got higher, like he was about to cry.
No— he wouldn't, right? Not Mickey.
But his breath had that
that sort of scratch.
"Why do I do that?"

I tried to speak but failed.
There wasn't anything I could do.

He raised his head. His eyes landed on me.

"No. I know what it is."
I stared back at him—
"I like it," he said. "I enjoy it. I like hurting myself."
—pretending I was older and knew better, I told him,
"You don't mean that."
"Look at me!"
It was a shout. It startled me.
There's something about being alone in a room with a man who's yelling
that just flat out feels unsafe, no matter who it is.
He noticed me flinch I think.
And his face softened.

"Look at me," he repeated.
Quieter,
a correction.
He motioned to himself,
to all of him.
And he was right.
There was the proof.

I dropped my head.
Crossed my arms.
The silence lasted, and he was done.
My turn.
I knew what I wanted to say
and I knew he wouldn't take it, just as he refused comfort the whole
night thus far.
But I'd say it and I'd be heard.
Maybe the next morning, with a more sane
less junk-food-fueled mind
he'd think it over and comprehend it.

"I've noticed," I said.
He tucked his chin.
"You do hurt yourself, and I didn't really realize it before tonight, but
in little ways, all the time, you do
Things that you think other people won't see, probably
Things you think they won't care to see.
I remember, the one time you went to the annual party at aunt Helen's
house—
it was just you and me and uncle David at the fire pit
We were making s'mores
And my marshmallow fell into the coals,
you picked it out with your bare hand"

(I remembered the way it looked when it happened,
the flames washing over his fingers like water
I thought it was brave,
I asked him if he was hurt, if he was okay,
he'd answered that it felt like nothing at all
and he handed the inedible, blackened marshmallow back to me like a
present

I couldn't refuse it after that
I held it the rest of the night)

"At the time I thought nothing of it," I continued, "but I know you better
now
and I know how you
get cracked hands in the winter and pick the scabs until they all bleed,
make jokes about yourself that I don't even know how to laugh at,
kick the ground when you're frustrated
hit the steering wheel when you miss a turn
And when you seem to be doing well, you do something strange like
how you pissed off aunt Helen five years ago and she cut contact with
you
And now this.
Quitting your job.
And the bad thing you still haven't told me.
Maybe the reason you do it is
you think you deserve to be unhappy.
Well, I don't believe that."
I slid off the counter and stood in front of him.
"People have been shitty to you."

His voice was low. "I've been shitty to people."
"Maybe," I said. "But you're not evil. And you deserve help, even if you
do something stupid.
That's what family is supposed to be there for, but ours is really, really bad
at making people feel like they belong, especially those who don't follow
the norm.
I sure don't— and I'm *way* worse than you,
I didn't go to college, I'm broke,
have no hope of getting married,
so help me God I'm never having kids—

By all their standards, I'm a loser.

"I don't feel welcome at my own parent's dinner table, let alone with the
whole family at thanksgiving,
as grandpa talks about how 'the homosexuals are corrupting the country'
and 'this generation is going to hell'
And God only knows all the racist shit and
and flat earth and
political conspiracy theories
but I keep my mouth shut. That's the only reason they keep me around,
because
you know both of us would be in the same boat if I did what you did.
But I'm not brave, like you.
That took some serious guts to tell them, despite the consequences
And I know you beat yourself up over it,
and you think you'd be better off if you never said a thing,
and maybe things would be easier, sure,"
I took a breath.

"But seeing...
someone who's like me
an adult who's kind and smart and doing just fine
someone who's not afraid to admit to who he is—

that meant the world to me.

And I appreciate it more than
you know, to know
that there's at least one person who would accept me and
not judge me for the way that I am.
I don't know how long it would have taken me to accept myself
if you didn't prove first

that it's possible.
Maybe that doesn't at all make it worth it to you, that's okay, I don't think
it does either,
but at least you can know it wasn't all bad.

"And I'm sorry they speak badly of you.
And I wish they didn't make you feel like the black sheep.
And I'm sorry no one wants to be around you anymore.
But I think, deep down, in their own way, they love you."
My words seemed to have no affect on him
as his unchanging face
remained drawn.
"I guess I can only speak for myself," I said.
"I l... I like you. And I care about you. And I want to be around you."

My words sat stale in the air for a horrible few seconds
and I began to think I had said something wrong.

He scoffed. "That sure means a lot, doesn't it?"

I was dumbfounded.
"What?"
He looked at me stupidly.
As I processed what he said, my breath was immediately choked and
got faster
"Was that sarcasm? What did you mean by that?"
He didn't give me the respect of replying.
"So it doesn't mean anything to you because— you need someone more
successful and more impressive than me to care about you.
Because I'm a failure too?
Love from a person like me isn't good enough?"

Love? Why did I say love?
I was embarrassed
My brain started going crazy
I was tired
I wanted to cry

I did cry.

"I didn't say that..." he said
Sheepishly. Pathetically.
That disgusted me.
And suddenly I forgot why I ever tried to help him.
Tears dropped down my face and I didn't wipe them.
"You're a jerk! No wonder everyone hates you. You're so wrapped up in
your self pity and your self loathing that you can't see anything. You can't
appreciate what you *do* have. And you do have an ego— all you *think*
about is yourself. You're a narcissist!"
I couldn't control myself anymore, I let out a sob
I covered my face and walked out of the kitchen
in a blur.

"Rose."
I heard him follow me.
I didn't care, I was leaving.
Forget the Chinese leftovers. He could have it. Let him include it in his
binge
fucking slob.
"Going home," I said.

"No, no — you're right about me!"
I turned, I looked at him, but I barely wanted to
He spoke in a panic

"You're right, I'm an asshole, and I'm sorry it took you that long to see it."
shaking his head and eyes darting around
his voice broke
"I'm stupid. I'm mean. And I'm not worth anyone's time. I'm not worth
your time."

I groaned. "Mickey! Insulting yourself is not an apology!"
I noticed he had teared up
I don't know when that started, but his eyes were red
and his hands went all nervous and jittery.
"I have a problem."
"Yes, you do," I answered.
"I'm sorry."

I sniffed and wiped my nose on my sleeve.
"Okay."
I didn't say 'it's okay,' because it wasn't.
"D-don't cry, please," he said, in a warbling voice
I just shook my head.
"Please. I'm sorry. Can I fix it?"
I didn't know how he could fix it now.
"You hurt me," I said. "I listened to you all night, I tried so hard for you,
and you just spit on it."
"I didn't mean to. I, and I know this is stupid, but when people say good
things about me, I think they're lying, I... didn't believe you."
"You're right, that *is* stupid."
"I'm sorry. I'm bad at reading people."
"You don't know how to listen!"
"I don't.
I don't.
I'm trying."
"Try harder!"

"Tell me what to do." He held out his hands like a man at the end of all things.

How could I explain?
I couldn't tell him.
He just had to know.
His hands fell to his sides
and when he saw that I couldn't give or wouldn't give an answer
he covered his face.
He wasn't ashamed.
Not quite.
Maybe just sad.

"Okay," he said.
He turned away.
"I understand."
I didn't really know what he meant.
"Thank you,"
he said.

My face tightened in confusion.
But then I got it.
my God,
He was an idiot.
Why did I care so much.

I quit crying, like a big girl
and stood straight
with determination.
"I want a hug," I said.
"Oh,"
He sort of prepared himself by facing me

"ohhkay, cool," he said.
I snorted a nasty post-blubbering laugh. "Weird thing to say."
And then I did hug him.

I expected him to be bad at hugging, if that makes sense
because yes, it's possible to be bad at it,
I certainly am
what with
never knowing how close to stand
where my arms should be, up, around, diagonal
or how long and how strongly to hold
and because he was so awkward about it
and so was I, I always am awkward about those things
never knowing who and when is appropriate.
It's weird with non-immediate family, like
my parents and brother, I always know how to hug them
but with cousins, aunts, uncles,
there's an unspoken
keep it quick rule
it has to be a side hug
barely even a hug
and in my family particularly (I think it's an Italian thing) a 'muah' sound
like a fake kiss on the cheek, but you don't actually touch faces
But Mickey broke all the rules immediately
He folded his arms so slowly around my back
It felt more like a hug
from a friend.

It was comforting, even though he smelled bad
(Mostly like pizza)
(But maybe I only think that because I hate pizza)
(I know, I know, call the cops)

And I felt safe, even though he was usually so unpredictable,
it felt secure
warm
Just the right amount of gentle.
And he didn't let go.

I held him tight in a way that meant,
'I'm still mad at you but everything's gonna be fine.'
And I asked a question with my voice muffled in his sleeve.
"So you didn't say that because I'm a loser?"
"No, no, I wouldn't think that about you."
"But I am, aren't I?"
"No."
I believed him.
After all,
I usually did.

He pulled away, but still held my shoulders.
"Love you."
It caught me off guard,
I lagged.

I imagine, when someone shows affection,
that if I return it
it won't be correct, I'll misunderstand
And they'll laugh or get mad at me
for doing it wrong, for making it weird.
I stared up at him
making sure I heard him right.
"Love you too."

He dropped his hands.

"Is this awkward?" He asked with a grimace.

I smiled. "A little."

He laughed and then showed his self soothing tic, hand around the back of his neck. "Sorry."

"No, it's my fault."

"Well I probably scared you off tonight, didn't I?"

"I actually had fun until just now."

"I had to go and ruin it."

A bit of silence as he switched back and forth between looking at me and not looking at me.

Then, embarrassed, "oh. I'll, I'll let you go now."

"Actually—" I interlaced my fingers behind my back. "Could I stay a little longer?"

"What— you want to? I thought you were leaving."

"I just said that because I was angry."

"Aren't you still?"

I shrugged.

"Well you can stay, I don't mind. I mean, you know, go ahead."

"Thank you."

On the couch again, laying down
on my phone as he watched TV
I yawned.
10:59
11:00
I double yawned.
A second later he echoed it in subconscious response.

Fox News
flick
NBC
flick
TLC
flick
A whisper from Mick since the volume was low enough to allow it,
"What do you want to watch?"

I wrapped myself tighter in the blanket
like when I was little at my grandparents house.
"Anything is fine."
He didn't answer.
It landed on Disney. Some sitcom I didn't recognize, from after my time.
Did he choose that for me, or for himself?
I smiled.
Either way, I approved.

I thought about asking again.
What really-not-good thing had he done?
He better not have hurt himself. He better not have hurt someone else.
I looked up at him, hoping to find the answer in his face.
But no—
I was missing something in this little mystery

It had to do with quitting his job, that was, what did he say,
'Part of it?'
Yeah.
I nuzzled my head into the pillow and closed my eyes.
He was probably just cooking meth. And that was comforting.

Though the debate wasn't exactly settled, now was not the time to pry
the truth out of him.
It was time to say nothing.
And it was enough
just being in the same room.

The sound of the TV blended together in a pattern of waves, punctuated
by the laugh track
and for a few seconds I became aware
that my thoughts were folding into sleep
but I couldn't find the resolve to stop myself.
If Mickey noticed, he didn't care

because the next thing I heard was a buzz from my phone.
It alerted me to the dark and absent room.
I felt intensely alone
until I looked at the text, it was from him.
It read,
"Goodnight, I messaged your mom and told her you're here."
Oh, good.
And sure enough, like clockwork,
Ten messages from mom.
Ding, ding, ding
"You're still at uncle Mickey's? Are you driving home? Do you need me
to pick you up?"
I sighed and checked the time.

12:50

I silenced my phone.
Goodnight.

I wonder

In the shade I'm still sweating.
That's what I get for wearing long sleeves in the summer.

He likes to do that too
look at him, sitting there, all chill in a charcoal suit.
His collar is unbuttoned a little
he looks so damn cool.

He isn't saying much, today.
I find it funny—
find it frightening—
silence from a man who always speaks his mind.

I stare at him as he slurps his soda
before flipping the page of his book.
He usually doesn't care to read;
he mostly prefers TV.

I wish I could start a conversation, but I don't know what to say
He usually takes care of the conversation starting...
... and ending.
But I love that brutal honesty.
He always has something shocking and hilarious to say in his
matter-of-fact way.

Well, best not to distract him from his book
it's a rare sight,
kind of a lovely sight to see.
I force myself to look away
and back down at my laptop screen.

I'm supposed to be writing.
I'm supposed to be enjoying it.
I probably would be if it weren't an academic essay.
Formal writing always has to be forced.
It's mechanical. Soulless.

Paragraph break. State your case. Convince your imaginary readers of an argument you couldn't care less about.

I'd much rather write
words
that *punch*
That don't hold back
Find their way into the corners of your mind
Build up like ocean waves and,

crash

I want my head to spin with a story that controls me
possesses me and won't set me free.

I don't think he thinks like that.
I look up at him
he's chewing on his chapped bottom lip.
No, he doesn't need to write anything down.
Any crazy thought in that head of his
flies out into the world as soon as a sentence can form.
The man's mouth is a machine gun.

I catch myself smiling,
I'm not happy, I just find it funny

that he doesn't know
how much I wish I could be like him.
Of course he doesn't—
I never told him.

"Whatcha lookin' at, kid?"
He looks up at me from under his bushy gray brows.

"Sorry."
My face gets hot.
"You, I guess."

"Something wrong?"

"No.
I was going to ask you the same thing;
you're quiet."

He smiles.
"Yeah?"
It widens.
"Don't get used to it."

"I wouldn't want to."

"What do you mean?"

"I like when you talk."

He closed the book, caterpillar brows lifting.
Our expressions create a silent conversation.

"That was—what's the word?"
"Frank?"
"Sure. I didn't expect it."
"Neither did I."

He clears his throat.
"Well, thanks. You mean that?"

"'Course I do. Why wouldn't I?"

He sniffs a bitter laugh.

"'Cause I'm offensive and senseless and my grammar's never right.
I'm rude. I'm loud. I always interrupt.
I laugh at my own jokes— people don't like that.
Not to mention I'm shifty and cocky and I dress like it's the eighties."

"What does the way you dress have to do with anything?"

He takes a big gulp of soda and whacks the can on the table.
"No one wants to listen to a guy who looks like a used car salesman."

I think about it for a second.
"You know, I like all those things."

He doesn't seem to buy it.

"I really do," I continue.
"I think you're confident and charismatic,
and I think you dress cool."

"That's real sweet of you, kid.
Where's all of this coming from?"

"I just thought I should say it.
Speak my mind
like you do."

He grinned at me then, a smile so big it took over his entire face.
But then it fell a little.
"I'm glad," he says.
"I'm glad you told me. I needed it."

After another pause, I ask,
"So, *is* something wrong?"

Breakfast

The sun is reflecting off the hood of a car outside the window and
shining into my eyes.
As I squint, the light gets caught in my eyelashes and turns everything
golden.

I look up at him.
He doesn't have the same problem—or maybe blessing—
because his back is to the sun

He looks at me
over his glasses and the menu
and smiles politely,
happily unaware of the torture
he puts me through every time that gaze rests on me.

His right hand releases the menu
He reaches up,
with elegant fingers, removes his glasses to place them on the table
They shine in the rose-gold atmosphere.

He waits expectantly
expecting me to speak?
How can I, when nothing stands between me and his paralyzing eyes?

His smile broadens, and his air of ease almost makes me calm again,
at least calm enough for me to smile back and quickly look away
and pretend to occupy myself with the menu.
Blueberry pancakes, or eggs and toast?

I don't answer myself.

I'm distracted by the wall made out of a mirror that all diners have for
some reason.
I wonder why
To make the space feel more open?

I see that other me sitting there in that other diner
What is that other version of me thinking?
Probably the same question
Eggs or pancakes,
I ask myself again.

Once more, I give myself no reply
imagining myself walking into that inverted reality, like Alice through
the looking glass.
Could things be different on the other side?

Eggs or pancakes?
The question now shouts itself, I have to answer,
'Eggs, they're healthier.'
But when the woman comes to take my order, I request pancakes, as I
always knew I would.

Once the menus are gone,
he speaks in his elegant and
melodic
voice
I can't help but wonder
if he gets as nervous as I do around him.
If he does, he's certainly spectacular at hiding it.

We both dress up for every occasion,

so, there's no way to tell if he put any extra care into that
subtly patterned tie;
suspenders instead of a belt;
wintery, coordinated colors.
I ponder his barely-there expression.
I want him to tell me everything on his mind.

I envision it as a garden
Flowers growing, their petals are pages torn out of books
Some are pieces of scrap paper, or yellow sticky notes with nonsense
written on them
Some hold lengthy monologues he never spoke out loud.
How I'd love for him to hand me a bouquet—
I'd study them for hours.

Why do I feel he's so far out of my reach?
He sits across from me, but never any closer
I wish he'd move just a little bit
Closer
I lean in without realizing it
Just a little bit
Closer

And for the first time
in all the time that I've known him,
he pauses halfway through his sentence.

Apologetically, I move back.
But I don't look away, and neither does he.
"You were saying?" I ask, and unfortunately, he continues.

But for a moment, I thought I might have seen a hint of a question in his
eyes—
the same question that plagues me.
A choice.
A decision that I can't seem to make.

I could tell him how I feel.
And even if he felt the same, I doubt he'd be quick to admit it,
under the judging eyes of everyone I know
and everyone he knows
and if anyone should know...

Or I could wait for these feelings to go away.
If they ever go away.
Wait until the day I have to watch him leaving
Or until I leave, never admitting...
But let's be honest.

Time is running out, and so is my coffee.
I realize as we walk out that this is the time to tell him
I could grab his hand dramatically, compelling him to look at me.
I could call to him just before he hops in his car.
I could forget about words altogether and just kiss him in the parking lot.

But of course,
just as I expected,
I watched the moment pass me by.
I say goodbye to him, I watch him leave,
the words I want to say
ring in my head.

Maybe, in some alternate reality,
I ordered eggs instead of pancakes.
Maybe I was brave, and I told him how I felt.
But here, it seems, I always take the easy road.

I shade my eyes from the sun, hoping to see his car pull back in
I just want one more chance
Even if I won't take it.